These questions are answered by:

All your answers are not wrong
All your answers are not always right
All come from your bright or dark thoughts
All come truly, deeply from your heart and soul
And all come to define who you are at this very moment

DAY 1

What is the one thing that you wish someone would do for you?

DAY 2

What are you most excited about when working?

DAY 3

What is the best decision you have ever made in your life?

DAY 4

What is your advice to the younger generation?

DAY 5

Do you have any favorite books that influenced you? What are those?

DAY 6

What can you learn from this?

DAY 7

Do you have any favorite memories of your house?

DAY 8

What is the one thing you want?

DAY 9

If you had to do it all over again, would you? Why?

DAY 10

How do you deal with the truth?

DAY 11

If you could be yourself, would you and why?

DAY 12

What are some things you can work on to help you relax and feel more comfortable?

DAY 13

What is your favorite way to sleep?

DAY 14

List of things that go away with sleep

DAY 15

When was the last time you saw the sunset in your country?

DAY 16

What do you wish you had more of that you know you don't have?

DAY 17

What sort of things are you interested in?

DAY 18

If you could give away one thing to someone, what would it be?

DAY 19

Do you like yourself better than you think?

DAY 20

How do you expect to be remembered?

DAY 21

What do you say when people try to be funny to you?

DAY 22

What are some of the biggest hurdles standing in your way right now?

DAY 23

If you were to write a book, would it be fiction or non-fiction, what would the subject be? Who is your target audience?

DAY 24

How would you describe the feelings of self-doubt?

DAY 25

What makes you feel loved?

DAY 26

Why do you want to get the same experience?

DAY 27

How would you describe the feeling of being on the defensive?

DAY 28

Would you rather have won the Grey Cup or a Super Bowl? Why?

DAY 29

Tell a memory that you have with one of your grandfathers.

DAY 30

What makes you feel scared when you try something new?

DAY 31

What's the thing you love about your mother?

DAY 32

Say something about your current status.

DAY 33

List of things that have gone horribly wrong

DAY 34

If you had to choose one thing you could do right now that would make an immediate difference to the quality of your life and that would have no impact on anything else, what would you choose?

DAY 35

Write a list of people you are grateful for being or having had been in your life.

DAY 36

What's the strangest present you've ever received?

DAY 37

How was your first kiss like?

DAY 38

How do you feel about your own body and your health?

DAY 39

What is the best thing you've ever done?

DAY 40

What's the one bad decision you ever made?

DAY 41

What are some of your better qualities?

DAY 42

If you had to choose a word from a dictionary to describe what you've learned thus far, what word would it be?

What would you do if you were invited to two parties on the same day?

What's the worst thing you've ever done as a person?

What are the things you think you could have done that haven't already been done?

DAY 46

What do you remember about the last thing you said to your best friend?

DAY 47

What are you most proud of today?

DAY 48

Would you rather have half a million pre-written post-it notes for the hours of your real lifetime?

DAY 49

What was your favorite thing to collect as a child? Why?

DAY 50

How do you account for the dry spells?

DAY 51

Is it possible to live a normal life and not ever tell a lie?

DAY 52

If you had to choose one thing to put in your bag, what would it be?

DAY 53

If you had to choose one thing that you believe makes a good person, what would it be?

DAY 54

What were the most important aspects of that day that you remember?

DAY 55

What has been the biggest challenge and opportunity for you?

DAY 56

Do you consider going off the grid? Why?

DAY 57

How did you discover yourself?

DAY 58

What is the hardest thing to do during a breakup?

DAY 59

What will you do with your last bite of a sandwich?

DAY 60

What is the one thing you have to say to your child about love?

DAY 61

What did your father teach you?

DAY 62

What's the coolest thing you've ever done?

DAY 63

What is one thing people usually miss when they are trying to decide where to start a journey?

DAY 64

What's your greatest fear?

DAY 65

What can you do to address this?

DAY 66

What would you do if someone cheated on you?

DAY 67

If your life was changed by power, what would it feel like?

DAY 68

Why do you think it was such a bad idea?

DAY 69

How would you describe the feeling of being more than a person, far beyond everyone else?

DAY 70

Describe your most important possession

DAY 71

What is the one thing that can kill you?

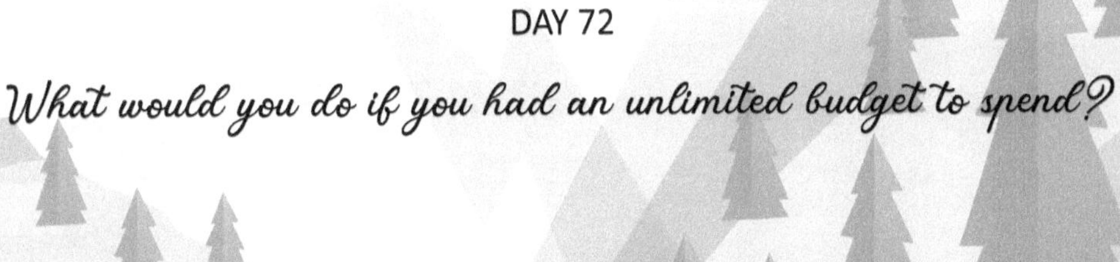

DAY 72

What would you do if you had an unlimited budget to spend?

DAY 73

Tell me about a 'perfect moment' you have experienced. Where were you, who was there, what happened, how did you feel? How does it feel remembering this moment?

DAY 74

Write about a dream you can remember.

DAY 75

If your stuffed animals could talk, what would they say?

DAY 76

How would you describe the feeling of being trapped?

DAY 77

What is your favorite film and why?

DAY 78

How do you deal with those feelings?

DAY 79

Explain pollution to a visitor from another planet.

DAY 80

Do you hate watching horror movies? Why?

DAY 81

When was the last time you ever got excited?

DAY 82

What is one thing you can learn from that whole experience?

DAY 83

What do you like to wear?

DAY 84

What would you do if you could bring yourself to do anything you wanted?

DAY 85

Are you an emotional fan? Why?

DAY 86

List of things that can cause you excitement

DAY 87

Where do you think you will be in five years?

DAY 88

What can you do to protect yourself from this?

DAY 89

When was the last time you went to a wedding? How was it?

DAY 90

List of things that can be worked with

DAY 91

If you could change anything about school, what would it be?

DAY 92

What is your "Why?"?

DAY 93

Do you prefer to learn more about the history of a country or place? Why?

DAY 94

List of things that I want to get better at each time

DAY 95

If you could travel anywhere for the rest of your life, where would you choose?

DAY 96

What have you seen as negatives and positives in your day to day life?

DAY 97

How would you describe the feeling of ignoring all the positive experiences you have?

DAY 98

Describe when someone has done something very nice for you

DAY 99

What was the most fun you had this year?

DAY 100

What do you do with your downtime?

DAY 101

What is one thing that you like most about yourself?

DAY 102

What do you think of the word "fantasy"?

DAY 103

How would you describe the feeling in your hands?

DAY 104

Say something about your new relationship.

DAY 105

What are you passionate about but can't have?

DAY 106

What is the one thing you do not like about your workflow?

DAY 107

What is something you never do?

DAY 108

What is the most ridiculous thing I could ask of you?

DAY 109

What are the qualities you're looking for in someone you want to grow old with?

DAY 110

Which would you choose as a defense against it?

DAY 111

What are the potential consequences of failure?

DAY 112

What is the one thing you can do today to make the world a better place?

DAY 113

Would you rather have a little bit of it or have all of it? Why?

DAY 114

What did you say your name was? Tell me the story about your name?

DAY 115

Would you rather have a cat than the world?

DAY 116

In your opinion, what's the best book about you?

DAY 117

Describe various styles of shoes as well as reasons for their popularity.

DAY 118

What did you teach your children about respect and kindness?

DAY 119

How would you describe the feeling of being invulnerable?

DAY 120

If you could be someone else for just one day for a year, who would it be and why?

DAY 121

Would you rather die than give this power to anyone?

DAY 122

What do you think about as you are falling asleep?

DAY 123

What are some things that sound like compliments but are insults?

DAY 124

What was the best thing that happened to you personally that you can't change?

DAY 125

How much money do you think is enough to live comfortably happy on per month? Breakdown the details.

DAY 126

Does your heart throb with longing? Why? Why not?

DAY 127

What is the thing that scares you the most?

DAY 128

If someone's feelings were truly your feelings, would you take a very great risk with them? Why?

DAY 129

What do you do on a normal day?

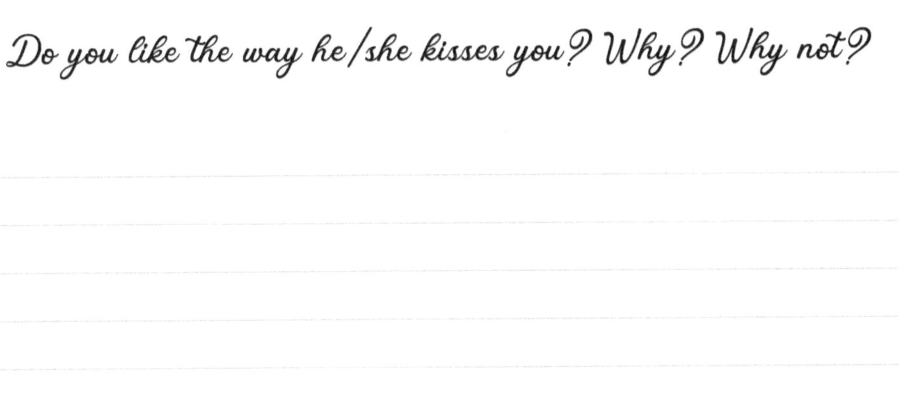

DAY 130

Do you like the way he/she kisses you? Why? Why not?

DAY 131

Do you want an active or passive lifestyle? Why?

DAY 132

What used to be considered trashy but now is very classy?

DAY 133

What would be your first order of business for today?

DAY 134

If you had to choose one of your favorite books of last year,
which book would it be and why?

DAY 135

How do you get out of here?

What challenges do you see in your community?

Do you feel mad when you feel sexy? Why?

Tell me, what is the last thing you want?

DAY 139

What do you think of your parents?

DAY 140

Would you rather be your own boss?

DAY 141

List of things that I should be doing

DAY 142

What is the most embarrassing thing you've ever say to
yourself?

DAY 143

When was the last time you were truly excited about a sports
game?

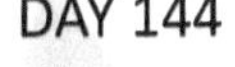

DAY 144

Who do you want to be happy with?

DAY 145

If you had to choose only one that would make you most happy, what would it be and why?

DAY 146

What do you think the secrets or keys to a happy life are?

DAY 147

What is the biggest challenge you're facing in your career or life?

DAY 148

Why do you think you're doing this?

DAY 149

How can you make it better than what it is now?

DAY 150

What causes you to stop and what causes you to pick your way back up?

DAY 151

What can you do to improve your image?

DAY 152

How would you describe the feeling of being relieved?

DAY 153

Talk about your favorite birthday celebration of all time.

DAY 154

How would you describe the feeling of being interrupted at every single point of time?

DAY 155

If you could pick one thing that you could say was the greatest game, what would it be?

DAY 156

What is the one thing that you feel you could've done differently in the past?

DAY 157

*Do you worry about losing yourself to the problem? Why?
Why not?*

DAY 158

If you could do it over again, which would you do?

DAY 159

What is the most rewarding thing you've ever done?

DAY 160

How would you describe the feeling of being judged?

DAY 161

What do you miss about your life?

DAY 162

How would you describe the feeling of being in a relationship
with a dead person?

DAY 163

What was your childhood favorite game?

DAY 164

When is a New Year's Eve you will never forget?

DAY 165

In what way do you prefer your job to be done?

DAY 166

Do you enjoy writing? Why or why not?

DAY 167

If you're a woman, what do you like about being a man?

DAY 168

*If you have the opportunity to travel to another planet, where
do you want to travel to?*

DAY 169

How do you deal with a situation like that when you have the experience that you have?

DAY 170

List of things that make you feel invincible

DAY 171

Would you continue? Why?

DAY 172

Tell me about a time when you took a big leap of faith or change of direction in your life. What motivated it?

DAY 173

If you could pick out one song that depicts how you want to be loved or depicts your ideal relationship, what is it and why?

DAY 174

What is the funniest joke you know by heart?

DAY 175

How do you deal with the stress that comes with trying to get your game on in the first place?

DAY 176

How would you describe the feeling of utter disappointment at being unable to help someone?

DAY 177

What are the three things you have that you believe in?

DAY 178

What is the best way to keep your friends on your trail?

DAY 179

What was the last holiday you went on?

DAY 180

What do you do when you're angry?

DAY 181

What if God would not judge us but you could, how would you
go about it?

DAY 182

Why do you keep saying that?

DAY 183

Who is the person you look up to?

DAY 184

What's your favorite kind of chocolate?

DAY 185

Tell about your home? Do you have a favorite room? Why?

DAY 186

How would you describe the feeling of being subjected to a task that your body does not understand?

DAY 187

How would you rate your most embarrassing story?

DAY 188

What is the best thing you have learned from that experience and what will you do differently next time around?

DAY 189

What's your favorite song to play in your car?

DAY 190

What is one thing you want to be remembered for?

DAY 191

What did you learn today?

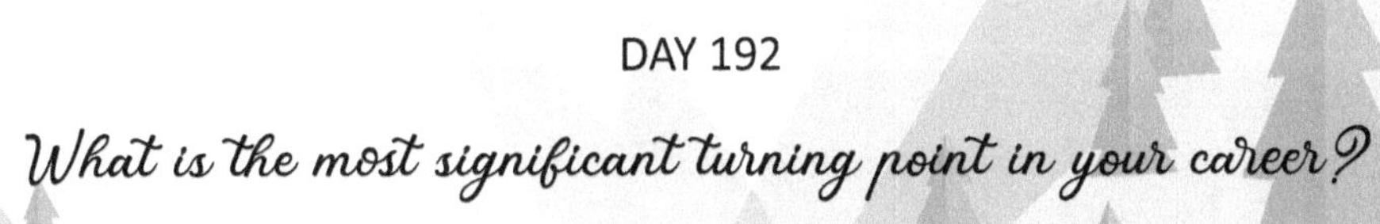

DAY 192

What is the most significant turning point in your career?

DAY 193

How do you deal with a world of a million species?

DAY 194

If you could change one thing in our world, what would it be?

DAY 195

Why do you think you can make the world a more meaningful place?

DAY 196

What was the worst childhood memory you have?

DAY 197

What is the best thing you can do to reduce your dependency on foreign dependencies?

DAY 198

List of things that you changed this week

DAY 199

What do you get after your job is done and you're free to be yourself for a bit?

DAY 200

What's the first step you can take to making a difference in the world today? Would you try to feed the hungry, improve the environment, promote peace? How would you start?

DAY 201

If you could teach someone how to ride a bicycle, would you and why?

DAY 202

What is most important to you to truly learn how to control your desires?

DAY 203

What ridiculous and untrue, yet slightly plausible, theories can you come up with?

DAY 204

You are a winner! How does it make you feel?

What is the most significant process you've had to overcome to improve your productivity?

What is one thing that you would like to be more known for?

What do you do when you're a horse?

DAY 208

How would you like to become famous?

DAY 209

Describe a time when you had to make a tough decision.

DAY 210

Would you rather not be able to read or not be able to write? Why?

DAY 211

How would you feel about it?

____

____

____

____

____

DAY 212

If you could change your name, would you want to and what name would you choose instead?

____

____

____

____

DAY 213

What causes you to feel pain even when you are conscious of that pain?

____

____

____

____

DAY 214

What are your happy thoughts?

DAY 215

What is one thing you wish you could do differently as a human being to make living more worthwhile?

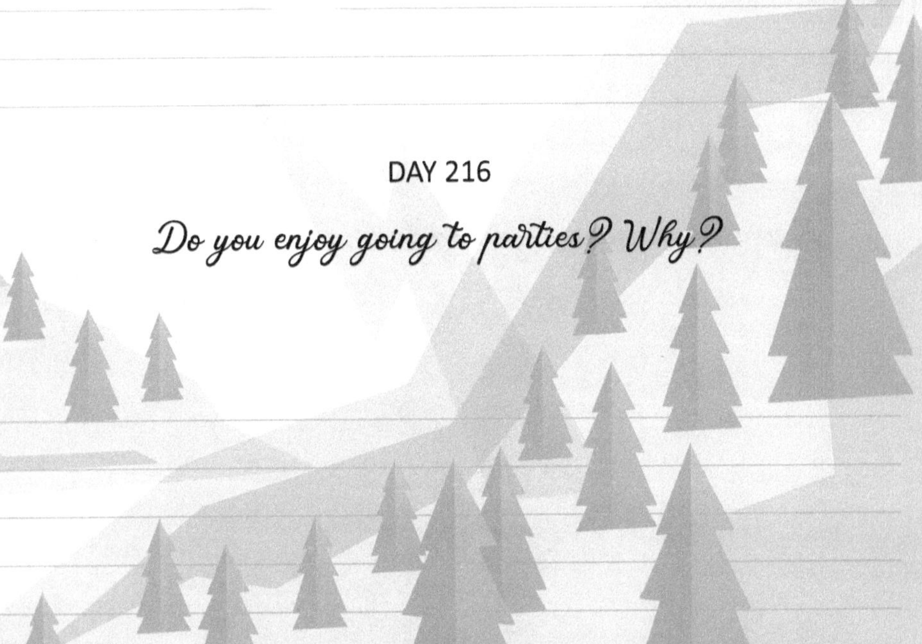

DAY 216

Do you enjoy going to parties? Why?

DAY 217

What is most important to your soul?

DAY 218

If you had to choose one thing that defines the future of the Internet, what would it be?

DAY 219

If you could have anything to lose, what would it be?

Think of your favorite toy. Why do you like it best?

DAY 221

What is your biggest worry?

DAY 222

If you could be any type of creature, which type would you be?

DAY 223

*If you had to live out your dream, would you be happy?
Why?*

DAY 224

What if all the streets were rivers? What would be different?

DAY 225

Discuss the importance of pride in one's work.

DAY 226

Why are you looking?

DAY 227

*If you could be playing for any team in the world right now,
who would it be and why?*

DAY 228

Say something about your true feelings

DAY 229

What would really help you right now?

DAY 230

What did you find in your research?

DAY 231

If you could get your life back, what would you want to change?

DAY 232

What is the one thing you say to make someone smile?

DAY 233

When did the world become so weird?

DAY 234

List of things that came to your mind first

DAY 235

*Have you ever seen something so beautiful it makes you cry?
Tell about it.*

DAY 236

*What do you remember about you and your grandfather or
grandmother?*

DAY 237

*Do you feel like people still have a sense of kindness these
days? Why?*

DAY 238

If you could go back and live a life in the past, would you do anything differently?

DAY 239

What was your New Years Resolution this year?

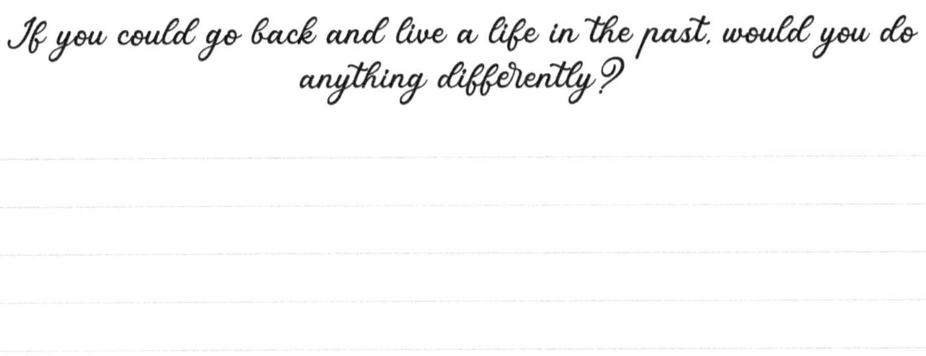

DAY 240

What have you been up to this year?

DAY 241

How many projects do you have on your "to-do" list?

DAY 242

What is your favorite dish around the world?

DAY 243

What is the one thing you need to achieve now that's not achieved already? What are you waiting for?

DAY 244

How do you get someone to like you?

DAY 245

What's the most fun thing you've done?

DAY 246

How do you deal with people who are not willing to acknowledge who they are?

DAY 247

What is the one thing you will always forget to take out?

DAY 248

What is your point?

DAY 249

What is your favorite type of perfume? Why?

DAY 250

Do you have a fear of failing at something? Why?

DAY 251

What did you do that was such a crime?

DAY 252

Tell a memory that you have with one of your grandmothers.

DAY 253

What is the worst thing you have ever seen done?

DAY 254

How do you cope with other friends that want to feel involved in the conversation but you know you can't because you're being very unhappy?

DAY 255

How would you describe the feeling of being dirty?

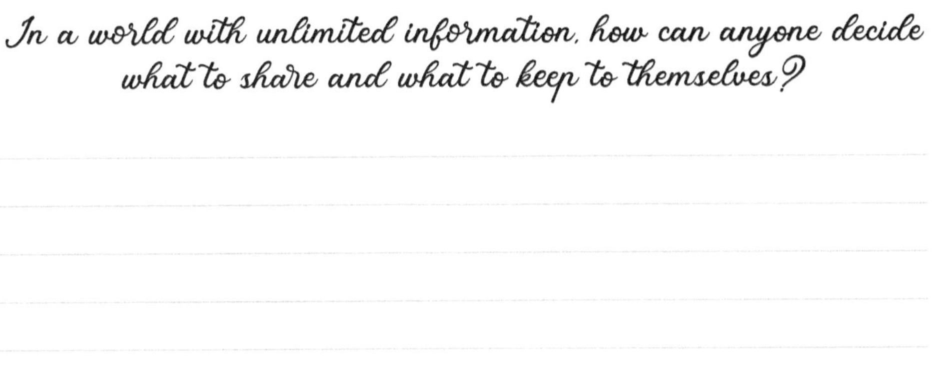

DAY 256

In a world with unlimited information, how can anyone decide
what to share and what to keep to themselves?

DAY 257

What is something you are optimistic about?

DAY 258

What if you lived your life in reverse like being born old
first?

DAY 259

Talk about your first kiss.

DAY 260

What do you love about your story?

DAY 261

How many hours does it take you to shower, wash your hair and iron your clothes?

What is the one thing you love most about life?

What can you bring to the table to make a difference?

You are now looking to become a better person each day, what is your goal for the day?

DAY 265

Why do you think you'll be able to take them?

DAY 266

Tell me about one of your favorite memories from the past year.

DAY 267

Do you think it's okay to keep secrets? Why?

DAY 268

Would you rather play as an evil scientist going from one maze to another or an evil doctor trying to cure people? Why?

DAY 269

List of things that I want to know how he became one of the best of all time

DAY 270

Would you rather always have your favorite song stuck in your head forever or always dream the same thing at night? Why?

DAY 271

If you had to choose one thing, would it be more on the dark side or on the light side?

DAY 272

When you were a kid, did you want to spend your time drawing?

DAY 273

Why do you say it's not a secret?

DAY 274

If you had to choose one thing in this world for yourself, what would it be?

DAY 275

Can you change? Why? Why not?

DAY 276

If you had to put pick a number that has most significance in your life, what will it be and why?

DAY 277

If you could save one animal, which one would it be and why?

DAY 278

If you could make one change in the world, what would it be?

DAY 279

If you had to choose a single song as your theme, what would it be?

What is the one thing you can see that doesn't matter?

Do you think that's enough? Why?

If you had to choose only one video to share with your friends and family this week, what would it be?

DAY 283

List of things that say the same thing

DAY 284

List of things that I want to investigate more

DAY 285

What were the most important lessons you learned from the journey?

DAY 286

If you could only have one thing for the rest of your life, what would it be?

DAY 287

How do you stay honest when in a situation where you have conflicting feelings?

DAY 288

What is the most exciting thing about your current job?

DAY 289

How would you describe the feeling of being scared that what you are doing is wrong?

DAY 290

How do you deal with criticism, especially when it's a good idea?

DAY 291

What is the most significant difference between your friends?

DAY 292

What is one thing you do not have?

DAY 293

Do you prefer dating just one person and see where it goes or dating multiple people until you make a decision?

DAY 294

What causes you to be so upset with someone?

DAY 295

What is the one thing that makes you super happy right now?

DAY 296

What is your biggest challenge to getting something done?

DAY 297

Say something about what you are going to do next.

If you had to choose one thing you'd like to see in the future,
what would it be?

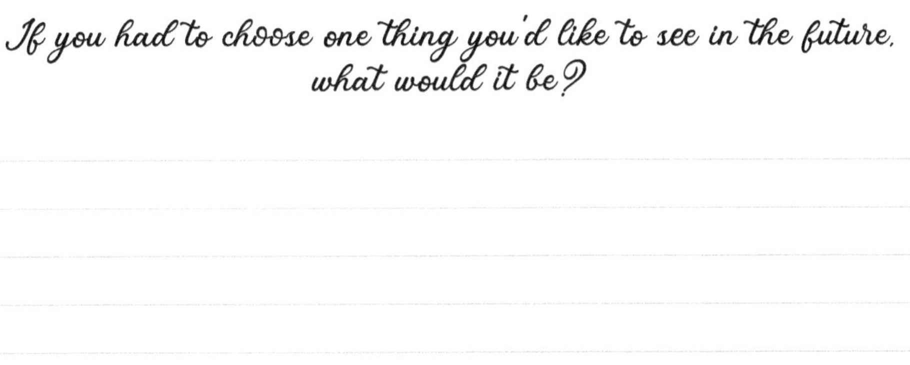

What is the quality you like most in a woman?

What if you can no longer see? What would you do?

DAY 301

What is the most annoying thing in a conversation?

DAY 302

Would you put your family or your friends first if you had to choose one?

DAY 303

How would you describe the feeling of being inside the box?

Things that would surprise you

List of things that have been considered punishment

What would make you feel more confident about you being able to handle it?

DAY 307

Would you rather the man be a coward than a fool, with an uncertain prospect and an uncertain future?

DAY 308

How did you get the right attitude and motivation?

DAY 309

If you had to look in a mirror reflectively, what would you see?

DAY 310

What are three things you are doing right now that make you different from everybody else?

DAY 311

If you had to choose to have one accessory, what would it be and why?

DAY 312

If you were given the choice between having three pairs of underwear to wear for the rest of your life, what would you choose?

DAY 313

What is the most significant problem facing the universe today?

DAY 314

What would you do if you suddenly discovered you didn't have a nose?

DAY 315

How would you describe the feeling of being absorbed in your work?

DAY 316

Where would you go to relax and why?

DAY 317

What's your mentality now?

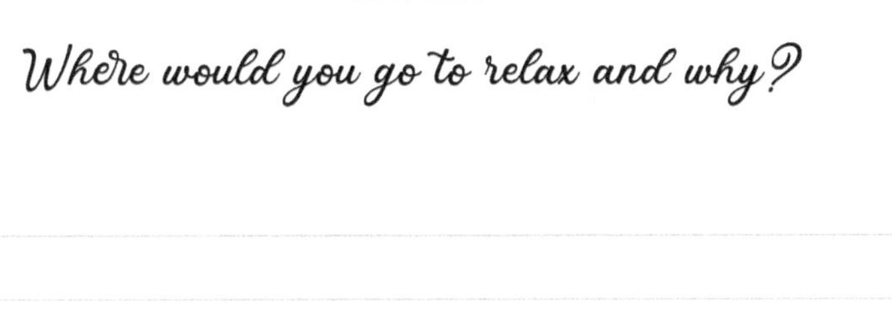

DAY 318

If you had to choose one thing from the past decade that has changed or grown you most, what would it be?

DAY 319

Which is most important to you, being popular, accomplishing
things or being organized and why?

DAY 320

Would you rather have a dog that can read your thoughts or
write what you want?

DAY 321

What do you hope never changes?

DAY 322

What did you think?

DAY 323

What do you think makes a good friend?

DAY 324

Do you find yourself in a constant search for things that are important to you in life? why?

DAY 325

Say something about you that won't make someone break up

DAY 326

Do you believe in magic? Why? Why not?

DAY 327

If you could go back in time to anything from your past, when would it be and what would you want to know about it?

DAY 328

If you are married, what's your first impression of it?

DAY 329

What do you do when you are out of money?

DAY 330

What is the one thing you wish the most for in the world?

DAY 331

What is your biggest dream?

DAY 332

What if someone gives you $100,000? What would you do with it?

DAY 333

How do you deal with a situation where you might have a lot of bad stuff going on but are still not prepared enough?

DAY 334

What are your fears being led?

DAY 335

Would you rather live a day in a man's heart or a thousand years in his thoughts?

DAY 336

What's a great thing for you to write about?

DAY 337

What happens if an obstacle must be cleared before a reward
can be received?

DAY 338

What should you look forward to in the future that you are not
doing now?

DAY 339

Would you rather spend your energy trying to unlock other ability than
dwelling on the major problems you'd encountered in the past?

How would you describe the feeling of being down and out and
getting every favor you can?

When was the last time you were in a group of friends
laughing together?

What does all this talking about mean about you?

DAY 343

Why do you want so much?

DAY 344

What you don't like about your face?

DAY 345

What are your worst qualities?

DAY 346

What can you do to ensure a smooth transition?

DAY 347

What is the best advice that you've ever received?

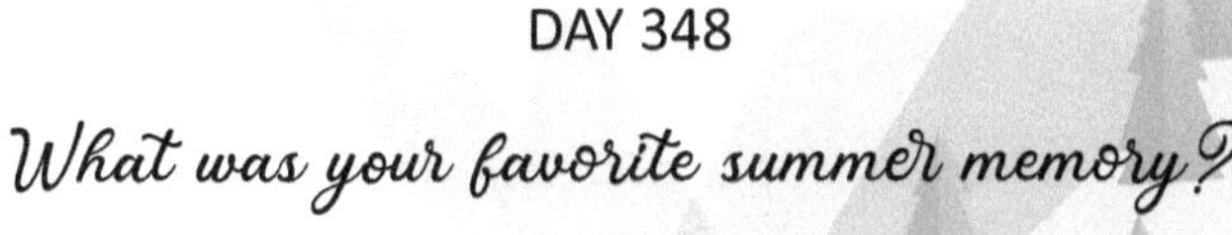

DAY 348

What was your favorite summer memory?

DAY 349

Tell how you can make a new friend.

DAY 350

What are your top three favorite technologies?

DAY 351

What fact do you try to ignore?

DAY 352

If you were forced to pick a superpower, which would you choose?

DAY 353

List of things that never hurt me for years

DAY 354

Have you ever had a wish that your beloved didn't fulfill? What was it?

DAY 355

Why is it important to be genuine?

DAY 356

What is your favorite song from a movie?

DAY 357

Would you rather be the author of your own reality or a participant in someone else's?

DAY 358

List of things that you want to say to anyone

DAY 359

Did you have to adapt to your new environment? Why?

DAY 360

How would you describe the feeling like "all my friends hate me and I feel like they don't even notice me"?

DAY 361

How would you describe the feeling of being judged and put down by people?

DAY 362

What is the biggest mistake you've made?

DAY 363

What are the benefits of having a sense of humor?

DAY 364

Is it easy for you to show yourself love or speak kindly to yourself?

DAY 365

What do you do to feel good about yourself?

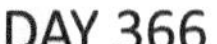

DAY 366

Do you feel sad when you don't do anything? Why?